# CONTENTS

# CLICKS AND ALGORITHMS: PROFITING FROM AI IN THE DIGITAL WORLD

Tiki Harmon

# THE AI REVOLUTION IN ONLINE BUSINESS

In the ever-evolving realm of technology, Artificial Intelligence (AI) has emerged as a transformative force, particularly in the sphere of online business. This revolution is not just a fleeting trend but a fundamental shift in how businesses operate, interact with customers, and envision the future. The journey of AI, from a concept in science fiction to a pivotal tool in digital commerce, is a testament to human ingenuity and the relentless pursuit of innovation.

## *Introduction to AI and its Impact on the Digital Landscape*

The story of AI begins with an understanding of its essence. AI, at its core, is the simulation of human intelligence processes by machines, especially computer systems. These processes include learning, reasoning, problem-solving, perception, and language understanding. In the digital landscape, AI has become synonymous with efficiency, personalization, and foresight.

The integration of AI into the digital world marked a significant shift in user experience. Online platforms began using AI for personalization, tailoring user experiences based on individual preferences and behaviors. Predictive analytics, powered by AI, enabled businesses to anticipate customer needs and offer relevant products and services. In digital marketing, AI transformed how brands engage with their audience, making marketing campaigns more targeted and effective. E-commerce platforms leveraged AI for various purposes, from chatbots that provide customer service to automated warehouses that streamline logistics.

However, the rise of AI also brought ethical and societal implications. The debate around AI ethics, particularly concerning data privacy and the potential for AI to perpetuate biases, became a focal point of discussion. The impact of AI on employment, with fears of job displacement, also became a significant concern. Des pite these challenges, the digital world continued to embrace AI, driven by its potential to revolutionize industries.

## Historical Evolution of AI in Online Business

The historical evolution of AI in online business is a narrative of gradual advancement and pivotal breakthroughs. Initially, AI's application in business was limited, more a subject of academic interest than practical use. However, the transition from theory to practice began as businesses started to recognize AI's potential.

The early stages of AI in business were marked by simple applications, such as basic automation and data analysis tools. These initial steps were crucial in demonstrating AI's viability in a business context. The real game-changer, however, was the advent of machine learning and big data. The ability of machines to learn from data and improve over time without explicit programming was revolutionary. Big data provided the fuel for AI's growth, offering the vast amounts of information needed for AI systems to learn and evolve.

This period also saw key milestones and case studies that shaped the future of AI in business. Pioneering companies, such as Amazon and Google, began to invest heavily in AI, integrating it into various aspects of their operations. These early adopters not only reaped significant benefits but also paved the way for others to follow. However, the journey was not without its failures. Some businesses rushed to adopt AI without a clear strategy or understanding of its capabilities, leading to costly mistakes and lessons learned.

## Overview of AI's Current Role and Potential Future Developments

Today, AI's role in online business is more significant than ever. Its applications span a wide range of industries, from retail and finance to healthcare. In retail, AI is used for personalized recommendations and inventory management. In finance, AI assists in fraud detection and algorithmic trading. In healthcare, AI aids in diagnostic procedures and patient care management.

The current landscape is also characterized by a global adoption of AI, with businesses around the world leveraging AI technologies to stay competitive. This widespread adoption, however, varies in scale and sophistication. While some regions and industries are at the forefront of AI integration, others are just beginning their journey.

Looking to the future, the potential developments of AI in online business are both exciting and daunting. Emerging trends, such as AI in blockchain technology, quantum computing, and advanced neural networks, promise to further enhance AI's capabilities. Predicting the next big thing in AI is challenging, but it is clear that AI will continue to be a major driver of innovation in online business.

As businesses prepare for an AI-driven future, they face both challenges and opportunities. One of the biggest challenges is the AI talent gap, with a shortage of skilled professionals to develop and manage AI systems. However, this also presents an opportunity for education and training programs to fill this gap.

In conclusion, the AI revolution in online business is a story of transformation, challenges, and endless possibilities. As AI continues to evolve, it will undoubtedly shape the future of online business in ways we can only begin to imagine. The journey of AI, from a nascent technology to a cornerstone of digital commerce, is a remarkable testament to the power of human innovation and the endless potential of technology.

# UNDERSTANDING AI: BASICS FOR DIGITAL ENTREPRENEURS

In the bustling digital marketplace of the 21st century, a new player has emerged with the potential to redefine the rules of the game: Artificial Intelligence (AI). For digital entrepreneurs, understanding AI is not just a luxury; it's a necessity to stay competitive and innovative. This story unfolds the layers of AI and machine learning, exploring their types and impacts, particularly in online business.

## *The Dawn of AI in Digital Entrepreneurship*

The journey into AI begins with its fundamental concepts. AI, in its essence, is about creating machines that can mimic human intelligence. This includes learning from experiences, understanding complex content, engaging in various forms of communication, and solving problems efficiently. Machine Learning (ML), a critical subset of AI, takes this a step further. It involves algorithms that enable computers to learn from and make decisions based on data, rather than following explicitly programmed instructions.

For digital entrepreneurs, this means an opportunity to harness a technology that can learn, adapt, and potentially outperform human capabilities in certain tasks. The implications are vast and varied, from automating mundane tasks to analyzing complex data sets for strategic insights.

## Types of AI in Online Business

As we delve deeper into the AI landscape, we encounter various forms that are particularly relevant to online businesses: chatbots, algorithms, and analytics.

- **Chatbots**: These AI-driven conversational agents have revolutionized customer service in the digital domain. They are programmed to mimic human conversation, enabling businesses to provide 24/7 support. Advanced chatbots are equipped with Natural Language Processing (NLP), allowing them to understand and respond to customer queries in a more human-like manner. For entrepreneurs, chatbots are not just cost-effective solutions but also tools for enhancing customer engagement and gathering valuable insights.
- **Algorithms**: The backbone of many online platforms, algorithms, powered by AI, are used for a range

of purposes from personalizing user experiences to optimizing operational processes. In e-commerce, for instance, AI algorithms analyze customer data to recommend products, predict trends, and manage inventory. For digital entrepreneurs, understanding and leveraging these algorithms can lead to more targeted marketing, efficient operations, and improved customer experiences.

- **Analytics**: AI-driven analytics transform vast amounts of unstructured data into actionable insights. This capability is invaluable for entrepreneurs in making data-driven decisions. AI analytics can identify patterns and trends that are not immediately apparent, offering a competitive edge in market analysis, customer behavior understanding, and strategic planning.

## *AI as a Game-Changer for Entrepreneurs*

The transformative power of AI for entrepreneurs lies in its ability to do things differently and more efficiently. AI opens up new avenues for innovation, customization, and scaling up operations.

- **Innovation**: AI encourages a culture of innovation. By automating routine tasks, it frees up entrepreneurs to focus on creative and strategic aspects of their business. AI can also drive product development, helping create new offerings tailored to customer preferences.
- **Customization**: Personalization is a key competitive advantage in the digital marketplace. AI's ability to analyze data at an individual level allows businesses to offer personalized experiences to their customers, from customized product recommendations to tailored content.

- **Scaling Operations**: AI can handle increasing volumes of work without the need for proportional increases in resources. This scalability is crucial for startups and growing businesses, allowing them to expand their operations without a corresponding increase in costs.

## Implementing AI in Business Strategies

For entrepreneurs eager to integrate AI into their businesses, the journey involves several steps. Identifying the right AI applications for their specific business needs is the first step. This could range from automated customer service systems to advanced data analytics tools.

However, implementing AI is not without challenges. Entrepreneurs must navigate issues such as data privacy, ethical considerations, and the potential impact on employment. Moreover, there's a need for a certain level of AI literacy to effectively manage these technologies.

As we look to the future, AI's role in business is set to grow even more significant. Entrepreneurs who embrace AI and learn to harness its full potential will find themselves at the forefront of the digital revolution.

## Conclusion

The story of AI in digital entrepreneurship is one of transformation, opportunity, and continuous evolution. From understanding its fundamental concepts to exploring its various applications, AI offers a new paradigm for how businesses operate and engage with their customers. For the digital entrepreneur, AI is not just a tool but a game-changer, offering new ways to innovate, customize, and scale. As AI continues to evolve, it will undoubtedly shape the future of online business in ways we are only beginning to imagine. The journey of AI, from a nascent technology to a cornerstone of digital commerce, is a remarkable testament to the power of human innovation and the endless potential of technology.

# AI AND THE FUTURE OF E-COMMERCE

In the dynamic world of e-commerce, a revolution is underway, driven by the power of Artificial Intelligence (AI). This story unfolds the transformative impact of AI on online shopping, inventory management, logistics, and predictive analytics, painting a picture of a future where AI not only enhances but redefines the e-commerce experience.

## *AI-Driven Personalization in Online Shopping*

The journey into AI's impact on e-commerce begins with personalization, a key area where AI has made significant strides. In the realm of online shopping, personalization is the cornerstone of customer experience. AI, with its ability to analyze vast amounts of data and learn from user interactions, has taken personalization to new heights.

Imagine an online shopping platform that not only knows your preferences but also anticipates your needs. AI algorithms analyze past purchases, browsing history, and even social media activity to understand individual customer preferences. This data is then used to tailor the shopping experience, offering personalized product recommendations, customized search results, and even individualized marketing messages.

For e-commerce businesses, AI-driven personalization means higher customer engagement, increased loyalty, and ultimately, enhanced sales. It's a win-win: customers enjoy a shopping experience that feels bespoke and intuitive, while businesses benefit from the increased efficiency and effectiveness of their marketing efforts.

## *Inventory Management and Logistics Optimization with AI*

Beyond the customer-facing aspects, AI's impact extends to the operational side of e-commerce, particularly in inventory management and logistics. In these areas, AI is a game-changer, enabling businesses to optimize their operations, reduce costs, and improve customer satisfaction.

In inventory management, AI systems predict demand for products with remarkable accuracy. They analyze trends, seasonal variations, and even external factors like economic indicators or social trends to forecast sales. This predictive power ensures that businesses maintain optimal inventory levels - enough to meet demand but not so much that it leads to overstocking and increased holding costs.

Logistics, the backbone of e-commerce, is another area where AI makes a significant impact. AI algorithms optimize delivery routes, reducing shipping times and costs. They also predict potential disruptions in the supply chain and suggest proactive measures to mitigate these risks. In warehouses, AI-powered robots work alongside humans to streamline the picking and packing process, increasing efficiency and reducing errors.

For e-commerce businesses, the benefits are clear: lower operational costs, improved efficiency, and enhanced customer satisfaction through faster, more reliable delivery.

## Predictive Analytics for Customer Behavior and Trends

Perhaps one of the most exciting applications of AI in e-commerce is predictive analytics. This involves using AI to analyze data and predict future customer behavior and market trends. Predictive analytics allows businesses to be proactive rather than reactive, anticipating changes in customer preferences and market conditions before they happen.

By analyzing data from various sources, AI can identify emerging trends, allowing businesses to adjust their strategies in real-time. This could mean stocking up on a product that is predicted to become popular, adjusting pricing strategies, or even developing new products to meet anticipated demand.

Predictive analytics also plays a crucial role in customer relationship management. By understanding customer behavior patterns, businesses can tailor their interactions with customers, offering personalized recommendations, promotions, and content that are more likely to resonate.

For e-commerce businesses, predictive analytics means staying ahead of the curve, adapting to changes in the market quickly, and maintaining a competitive edge.

## The Future of E-Commerce with AI

As we look to the future, the role of AI in e-commerce is set to grow even more significant. The integration of AI technologies like voice recognition and augmented reality into online shopping platforms will further enhance the customer experience. AI will also continue to improve operational efficiencies in inventory management and logistics, with advancements in robotics and autonomous vehicles.

However, this future also brings challenges. Issues such as data privacy, ethical use of AI, and the potential impact on employment in the retail sector will need to be addressed. Businesses will need to navigate these challenges carefully, ensuring that they use AI in a way that is ethical, responsible, and beneficial to both the company and its customers.

## Conclusion

The story of AI in e-commerce is one of transformation and endless possibilities. From personalizing the online shopping experience to optimizing inventory and logistics, AI is not just enhancing existing processes but creating new opportunities for innovation and growth. As AI continues to evolve, it will undoubtedly shape the future of e-commerce, offering a more efficient, personalized, and predictive shopping experience. For businesses and customers alike, the AI-driven future of e-commerce is bright, promising a world where shopping is not just a transaction, but an intuitive, seamless, and enjoyable experience.

# LEVERAGING AI FOR EFFECTIVE SOCIAL MEDIA MARKETING

In the dynamic world of social media marketing, Artificial Intelligence (AI) has emerged as a powerful ally for brands and marketers. This story explores how AI tools are revolutionizing content creation, audience targeting, and campaign management, illustrated through case studies of successful AI-driven campaigns.

## AI Tools for Content Creation and Scheduling

The first chapter in our AI-driven social media saga begins with content creation and scheduling. In the fast-paced social media landscape, creating engaging, relevant, and timely content is crucial. AI tools have transformed this process, making it more efficient and effective.

AI-powered content creation tools use natural language

processing (NLP) and machine learning algorithms to generate creative and engaging text, graphics, and video content. These tools analyze existing content trends and user engagement to suggest or even autonomously create content that resonates with the target audience. For instance, AI can generate variations of ad copy, test them in real-time, and determine which version performs best, all in a fraction of the time it would take a human team.

Scheduling is another area where AI makes a significant impact. AI-driven scheduling tools analyze data on when a brand's audience is most active and engaged, determining the optimal times for posting. This ensures that content reaches the maximum number of users, increasing engagement and visibility.

## Analyzing and Targeting Audiences with AI

The next phase in leveraging AI for social media marketing is audience analysis and targeting. Understanding and segmenting the audience is key to any successful marketing strategy, and AI takes this to a new level.

AI tools analyze vast amounts of data from social media platforms to gain insights into user behaviors, preferences, and trends. This analysis includes demographic information, engagement patterns, and even sentiment analysis to gauge user reactions to content and products. By processing this data, AI helps marketers create highly targeted and personalized marketing campaigns.

For instance, AI can identify micro-segments within a broader audience, allowing marketers to tailor their messages to specific groups. This level of personalization was once a time-consuming and complex process, but AI makes it fast and scalable.

## Case Studies of Successful AI-Driven Social Media Campaigns

To illustrate the power of AI in social media marketing, let's examine some case studies of successful AI-driven campaigns.

- **Case Study 1: AI-Powered Personalization** A leading fashion brand implemented an AI-driven marketing strategy on their social media platforms. Using AI, they analyzed customer data to create personalized product recommendations for each user. The AI system also optimized ad placements and timings based on user engagement patterns. The result was a significant increase in click-through rates and online sales, demonstrating the power of personalized marketing.
- **Case Study 2: AI for Real-Time Engagement** A technology company used AI to monitor social media conversations in real-time during a product launch. The AI tool analyzed user sentiments and identified trending topics, allowing the company to engage with users through timely and relevant content. This proactive approach led to a positive brand image and increased user engagement during the critical launch period.
- **Case Study 3: AI-Driven Content Strategy** A food and beverage company leveraged AI to analyze social media trends and user preferences. Based on this analysis,

the AI tool suggested content themes and formats that resonated with the target audience. The company used these insights to create a content strategy that significantly increased user engagement and brand loyalty.

## The Future of AI in Social Media Marketing

As we look to the future, the role of AI in social media marketing is set to grow even more significant. With advancements in AI technology, we can expect even more sophisticated tools for content creation, audience analysis, and campaign management. However, this future also brings challenges, such as ensuring data privacy and navigating the ethical implications of AI.

## Conclusion

The story of AI in social media marketing is one of transformation and innovation. From content creation and scheduling to audience targeting and campaign management, AI has not just enhanced existing processes but created new opportunities for creativity and engagement. As AI continues to evolve, it will undoubtedly shape the future of social media marketing, offering more efficient, personalized, and impactful ways to connect with audiences. For brands and marketers, embracing AI is no longer an option but a necessity to stay competitive in the ever-changing social media landscape.

# MASTERING AI IN SEARCH ENGINE OPTIMIZATION

I n the intricate world of digital marketing, Search Engine Optimization (SEO) stands as a critical pillar. The advent of Artificial Intelligence (AI) has revolutionized this domain, offering new tools and strategies to master SEO. This story delves into the role of AI in understanding search engine algorithms, enhancing keyword research, content optimization, and measuring SEO performance.

## *Understanding AI Algorithms in Search Engines*

The journey into AI-enhanced SEO begins with a fundamental understanding of AI algorithms in search engines. Modern search engines like Google have evolved far beyond simple keyword matching. They now employ sophisticated AI algorithms to understand and rank web content.

These AI algorithms are designed to mimic human

understanding, interpreting the intent behind a user's search query rather than just matching keywords. They analyze factors like context, content quality, user engagement, and website authority. For instance, Google's AI algorithm, RankBrain, uses machine learning to interpret search queries and deliver more relevant search results.

For SEO professionals, this means adapting to a landscape where keyword stuffing and traditional optimization techniques are no longer effective. Instead, the focus shifts to creating high-quality, relevant content that aligns with user intent and provides value.

## *AI Strategies for Keyword Research and Content Optimization*

The next chapter in AI-driven SEO is about leveraging AI for keyword research and content optimization. AI tools have transformed keyword research from a guessing game into a data-driven strategy. These tools analyze search trends, user behavior, and even competitor content to identify the most effective keywords.

AI-powered keyword research tools go beyond simple search volume data. They provide insights into the context, relevance, and competitiveness of keywords. This allows SEO professionals to target long-tail keywords and niche topics that offer higher conversion rates and less competition.

Content optimization with AI involves more than just

incorporating keywords. AI tools can analyze top-performing content across the web to identify patterns and elements that resonate with users. This includes content structure, tone, readability, and even multimedia elements. By applying these insights, SEO professionals can create content that not only ranks well but also engages and retains users.

## Measuring and Analyzing SEO Performance with AI Tools

The final piece of the AI-SEO puzzle is measuring and analyzing SEO performance. AI tools have revolutionized this aspect, offering more comprehensive and accurate insights into SEO campaigns.

AI-driven analytics tools track a wide range of metrics, from traditional rankings and traffic data to more nuanced indicators like user engagement and content relevance. They can identify which pages are performing well, which need improvement, and why. This level of analysis was once time-consuming and complex, but AI makes it fast and accessible.

Moreover, AI tools can predict how changes in SEO strategy will impact performance. They use historical data and current trends to forecast the outcomes of different SEO tactics, allowing professionals to make data-driven decisions.

## *The Future of AI in SEO*

As we look to the future, the integration of AI in SEO is set to deepen. We can expect even more sophisticated AI algorithms from search engines, requiring continuous adaptation and learning from SEO professionals. AI will also continue to evolve in keyword research, content optimization, and performance analysis, offering more precise and actionable insights.

However, this future also brings challenges. Staying updated with the latest AI advancements, ensuring ethical use of AI, and maintaining a balance between AI-driven strategies and human creativity will be crucial.

## *Conclusion*

The story of AI in SEO is one of continuous evolution and adaptation. From understanding complex search engine algorithms to enhancing keyword research and content optimization, AI has not just improved existing processes but has opened new avenues for innovation and success in SEO. As AI continues to advance, it will undoubtedly shape the future of SEO, offering more efficient, effective, and intelligent ways to optimize digital content. For SEO professionals, mastering AI is no longer an option but a necessity to stay ahead in the ever-changing landscape of digital marketing.

# CHATBOTS AND CUSTOMER SERVICE AUTOMATION

In the digital age, where instant gratification is the norm, Artificial Intelligence (AI) chatbots have emerged as a cornerstone in customer service automation. This story delves into the intricacies of designing and implementing AI chatbots, enhancing customer experiences, and integrating these digital assistants into various platforms like social media and websites.

## Designing and Implementing AI Chatbots

The journey into the world of AI chatbots begins with their design and implementation. Creating an effective chatbot is not just about programming responses but about understanding and anticipating customer needs. The design process involves several key steps:

- **Understanding Customer Needs:** The first step in designing a chatbot is to understand the customer's needs and the common queries they might have. This involves analyzing customer service data, identifying frequently asked questions, and understanding the customer journey.

- **Choosing the Right AI Technology**: The next step is selecting the appropriate AI technology. This includes deciding between rule-based systems, which follow predefined paths, and more advanced AI that uses natural language processing (NLP) to understand and respond to user queries in a more human-like manner.
- **Developing the Chatbot**: The development phase involves programming the chatbot with a set of responses and learning algorithms. This is where the chatbot is 'trained' with a variety of customer interactions to improve its understanding and response accuracy.
- **Testing and Iteration**: Before full deployment, chatbots undergo rigorous testing to ensure they can handle a wide range of queries accurately and efficiently. Continuous iteration and learning are key, as customer needs and behaviors evolve over time.

## Enhancing Customer Experience with Automated Responses

Once implemented, AI chatbots play a pivotal role in enhancing the customer experience. Their ability to provide instant, 24/7 responses transforms the way businesses interact with their customers.

- **Immediate Response**: In today's fast-paced world, customers expect immediate answers. Chatbots fulfill this expectation by providing instant responses to queries, reducing wait times and improving overall customer satisfaction.
- **Personalization**: Advanced AI chatbots can offer personalized experiences by remembering past interactions and preferences. This level of personalization makes customers feel valued and

understood, fostering loyalty and trust.

- **Handling High Volume**: Chatbots can handle a high volume of queries simultaneously, something that would be resource-intensive and costly with human agents. This scalability ensures that customer service quality doesn't diminish during peak times.

## Integrating Chatbots with Social Media and Websites

The true power of AI chatbots is realized when they are seamlessly integrated into platforms where customers are most active, such as social media and websites.

- **Social Media Integration**: Integrating chatbots with social media platforms like Facebook, Twitter, and Instagram allows businesses to interact with customers where they spend a significant amount of their time. These chatbots can handle queries, provide product recommendations, and even complete transactions within the social media platform.
- **Website Integration**: On websites, chatbots can offer immediate assistance to visitors, whether it's guiding them through the site, answering product-related queries, or assisting with purchases. This not only enhances the user experience but also increases the chances of conversion.

## *The Future of Chatbots in Customer Service*

Looking to the future, the role of AI chatbots in customer service is set to become even more integral. Advancements in AI and machine learning will enable chatbots to provide more nuanced and human-like interactions. The integration of chatbots with other emerging technologies like augmented reality (AR) and the Internet of Things (IoT) will further expand their capabilities.

However, this future also brings challenges. Balancing the efficiency of chatbots with the need for human touch in certain complex or sensitive situations will be crucial. Ensuring data privacy and ethical use of AI in customer interactions will also be paramount.

## *Conclusion*

The story of AI chatbots in customer service is one of innovation, efficiency, and continuous evolution. From their design and implementation to enhancing customer experiences and integrating with key digital platforms, chatbots have not just improved existing processes but have opened new avenues for customer engagement. As AI continues to advance, chatbots will undoubtedly shape the future of customer service, offering more intelligent, efficient, and personalized interactions. For businesses, leveraging the power of AI chatbots is no longer an option but a necessity to meet the evolving expectations of the digital customer.

# AI IN EMAIL MARKETING: PERSONALIZATION AND EFFICIENCY

In the ever-evolving landscape of digital marketing, Artificial Intelligence (AI) has emerged as a pivotal force, especially in the realm of email marketing. This story unfolds the journey of AI in revolutionizing email campaigns through automation, personalization, list segmentation, optimization of send times, and analysis of campaign effectiveness.

## *Automating and Personalizing Email Campaigns*

The first chapter in the AI-driven email marketing story is about automation and personalization. In an age where consumers are bombarded with generic marketing messages, personalization has become the key to capturing attention. AI steps in as a powerful tool to personalize email content at scale.

AI algorithms analyze customer data, including past purchases, browsing behavior, and engagement history, to create highly personalized email content. This goes beyond addressing the recipient by name; AI can tailor the entire email content to align with individual user preferences and behaviors. For instance, an AI system can automatically generate product recommendations based on a customer's browsing history or past purchases.

Moreover, AI-driven automation streamlines the email marketing process. It can autonomously design email campaigns, decide on the content, and even choose appropriate visuals, making the process more efficient and reducing the workload on marketing teams.

## AI for Segmenting Email Lists and Optimizing Send Times

Segmentation and timing are critical in email marketing, and AI significantly enhances these aspects. Traditionally, segmenting email lists was a manual and time-consuming process, based on basic criteria like demographics or past purchases. AI, however, takes this to a new level.

Using advanced data analysis, AI can segment email lists based on more nuanced criteria, such as user behavior patterns, engagement levels, and even predictive analysis of future needs. This results in more targeted and effective email campaigns, as messages are tailored to the specific needs and interests of different audience segments.

Optimizing send times is another area where AI excels. Instead of relying on generalized best practices, AI analyzes the engagement patterns of each recipient to determine the optimal time to send an email. This ensures that emails are more likely to be opened and read, increasing the overall effectiveness of the campaign.

## Analyzing Email Campaign Effectiveness with AI

The final piece of the AI in email marketing puzzle is analyzing campaign effectiveness. AI tools offer a more sophisticated analysis of email campaign performance, going beyond basic metrics like open rates and click-through rates.

AI systems can track and analyze user interactions with emails, providing insights into what content works and what doesn't. They can identify patterns in user behavior, such as which types of emails prompt more website visits or purchases. This level of analysis helps in refining email strategies, ensuring that future campaigns are more aligned with user preferences and behaviors.

Moreover, AI can predict the future performance of email campaigns based on historical data. This predictive analysis helps in making more informed decisions about email marketing strategies, optimizing for better results.

## The Future of AI in Email Marketing

As we look to the future, the integration of AI in email marketing is set to deepen. We can expect even more sophisticated personalization, with AI creating entirely unique email content for each recipient. The segmentation and timing of emails will become more precise, and the analysis of campaign effectiveness will offer even deeper insights.

However, this future also brings challenges. Ensuring data privacy and navigating the ethical implications of using AI in marketing will be crucial. Balancing the efficiency and personalization offered by AI with the need for a human touch in certain aspects of marketing will also be important.

## Conclusion

The story of AI in email marketing is one of transformation, efficiency, and continuous evolution. From automating and personalizing email campaigns to segmenting email lists and optimizing send times, AI has not just improved existing processes but has opened new avenues for innovation and success in email marketing. As AI continues to advance, it will undoubtedly shape the future of email marketing, offering more intelligent, efficient, and personalized ways to connect with audiences. For marketers, mastering AI in email marketing is no longer an option but a necessity to stay ahead in the competitive digital landscape.

# CONTENT CREATION WITH AI: BLOGS, ARTICLES, AND MORE

In the ever-expanding universe of digital content, Artificial Intelligence (AI) has emerged as a transformative force in content creation. This story explores the journey of AI in generating and curating content, the interplay between AI and human creativity, and the ethical considerations and quality control in AI-driven content creation.

## Using AI for Generating and Curating Content

The first chapter in our exploration of AI in content creation revolves around its capability to generate and curate content. AI, with its advanced algorithms and machine learning capabilities, has opened new avenues in content creation, particularly for blogs and articles.

AI-driven content generation tools use natural language processing (NLP) to create coherent, readable, and contextually relevant text. These tools can analyze existing content on a given topic, extract key information, and generate new content that aligns with the desired tone, style, and format. For instance, AI can be used to write news articles based on data inputs, create blog posts from outlines, or even generate entire ebooks.

Beyond generation, AI also plays a crucial role in content curation. AI algorithms can sift through vast amounts of online content to identify trends, popular topics, and emerging narratives. This capability enables content creators to stay ahead of the curve, producing content that resonates with current interests and demands.

## Balancing AI and Human Creativity in Content Creation

While AI brings efficiency and scalability to content creation, the role of human creativity remains paramount. The second chapter of our story focuses on finding the right balance between AI and human creativity.

AI is excellent at handling large-scale, data-driven tasks and can produce content quickly. However, it lacks the nuanced understanding and emotional depth that human creativity brings. The most effective content often comes from a collaboration between AI and human creators. AI can provide a foundation – generating initial drafts, suggesting ideas, or curating content – which human creators can then refine, add nuance to, and infuse with creativity and empathy.

This collaborative approach leverages the strengths of both AI and humans. AI handles the heavy lifting of data processing and initial content generation, while humans bring in critical thinking, emotional intelligence, and creative flair.

## Ethical Considerations and Quality Control

The final chapter in our AI content creation story addresses the ethical considerations and the importance of quality control. As AI becomes more prevalent in content creation, concerns about authenticity, transparency, and quality have emerged.

One of the primary ethical considerations is the transparency of AI-generated content. It's important for readers to know whether the content they're consuming was generated by AI. This transparency is crucial for maintaining trust and credibility.

Quality control is another significant aspect. While AI can generate content, it may not always meet the high standards required for accuracy, readability, and engagement. Human oversight is essential to ensure that AI-generated content is factually correct, well-written, and aligns with the brand's voice and values.

Moreover, there's a need to guard against the misuse of AI in content creation, such as generating misleading or biased content. Establishing ethical guidelines and quality standards is crucial to ensure that AI is used responsibly in content creation.

## *The Future of AI in Content Creation*

Looking to the future, AI's role in content creation is set to grow even more significant. We can expect advancements in AI technology to lead to more sophisticated content generation tools, capable of producing more nuanced and high-quality content. The collaboration between AI and human creators will also evolve, with new tools and processes emerging to streamline this partnership.

However, this future also brings challenges. Navigating the ethical implications of AI in content creation, ensuring quality control, and maintaining the right balance between AI and human input will be crucial.

## *Conclusion*

The story of AI in content creation is one of innovation, collaboration, and continuous evolution. From generating and curating content to balancing AI with human creativity, and addressing ethical considerations and quality control, AI has not just transformed existing processes but has opened new possibilities for creativity and efficiency. As AI continues to advance, it will undoubtedly shape the future of content creation, offering more intelligent, efficient, and collaborative ways to produce content. For content creators, embracing AI while maintaining human creativity and ethical standards is key to succeeding in this new landscape.

# DATA-DRIVEN DECISIONS: AI IN ANALYTICS

I n the modern business landscape, where data is as valuable as currency, Artificial Intelligence (AI) has become a key player in transforming data into actionable insights. This story delves into how AI is revolutionizing business intelligence, customer data analysis, and the tools and platforms that drive AI-powered analytics.

## *Utilizing AI for Business Intelligence and Decision-Making*

The journey into AI-driven analytics begins with its application in business intelligence and decision-making. In an era where businesses are inundated with data, AI emerges as a crucial tool for sifting through this information and extracting valuable insights.

AI algorithms, with their ability to process and analyze large datasets quickly and accurately, provide businesses with a deeper understanding of their operations, market trends, and customer preferences. This capability is not just about handling quantitative data; AI can also interpret qualitative data, like customer feedback, to provide a more holistic view of the business landscape.

For decision-makers, this means access to insights that were previously hidden in the vast sea of data. AI-driven analytics can identify patterns and trends that inform strategic decisions, from product development to market expansion strategies. For instance, AI can analyze market data to predict future trends, helping businesses stay ahead of the curve.

## Analyzing Customer Data for Insights and Trends

The next chapter in our AI analytics story focuses on customer data analysis. In today's customer-centric business environment, understanding the customer is key to success. AI plays a pivotal role in unraveling the complexities of customer data, providing insights into customer behavior, preferences, and needs.

AI algorithms can analyze customer interactions across various touchpoints – from social media to purchase history – to build comprehensive customer profiles. This analysis goes beyond basic demographics to include behavioral patterns and psychographic data.

The insights gained from AI-driven customer data analysis are invaluable. They enable businesses to tailor their products, services, and marketing efforts to meet the specific needs and preferences of different customer segments. For example, AI can identify which products are popular among certain demographic groups or which marketing messages resonate best with different audiences.

## Tools and Platforms for AI-Driven Analytics

The final piece of our AI in analytics story revolves around the tools and platforms that make AI-driven analytics possible. The market is replete with a wide range of AI analytics tools, each offering unique features and capabilities.

These tools range from comprehensive business intelligence platforms that provide end-to-end analytics solutions to specialized tools focused on specific aspects like customer sentiment analysis or predictive modeling. For instance, platforms like IBM Watson and Google Analytics leverage AI to provide deep insights into business and customer data.

Choosing the right tools and platforms depends on the specific needs and goals of the business. Factors to consider include the type of data being analyzed, the level of AI sophistication required, and integration capabilities with existing systems.

## The Future of AI in Analytics

As we look to the future, the role of AI in analytics is set to become even more integral. Advancements in AI technology will lead to more sophisticated analytics tools, capable of providing deeper and more nuanced insights. The integration of AI analytics with other emerging technologies like the Internet of Things (IoT) and augmented reality (AR) will further expand its capabilities.

However, this future also brings challenges. Ensuring data privacy and security, navigating the ethical implications of AI, and maintaining the accuracy and reliability of AI-driven insights will be crucial.

## Conclusion

The story of AI in analytics is one of transformation, innovation, and continuous evolution. From enhancing business intelligence and decision-making to unraveling customer data for insights and trends, AI has not just improved existing processes but has opened new possibilities for data-driven decision-making. As AI continues to advance, it will undoubtedly shape the future of analytics, offering more intelligent, efficient, and insightful ways to harness the power of data. For businesses, leveraging AI in analytics is key to staying competitive in a data-driven world.

# AI AND AFFILIATE MARKETING: A NEW APPROACH

In the dynamic and competitive realm of affiliate marketing, Artificial Intelligence (AI) has emerged as a game-changer, offering innovative approaches to selecting and promoting products, utilizing predictive analytics, and enhancing overall marketing strategies. This story delves into how AI is reshaping affiliate marketing, illustrated through case studies and practical insights.

## *AI for Selecting and Promoting Affiliate Products*

The first chapter in our exploration of AI in affiliate marketing focuses on the selection and promotion of products. Traditionally, selecting products for affiliate marketing involved manual research and often a bit of guesswork. AI, however, brings a data-driven approach to this process.

AI algorithms can analyze vast amounts of data from various sources, including market trends, consumer behavior, and past performance of products, to identify the most promising affiliate products. This analysis is not just limited to identifying popular products; it also considers factors like compatibility with the affiliate's audience, potential for long-term success, and even the likelihood of future market trends.

When it comes to promoting affiliate products, AI again plays a crucial role. AI-driven tools can optimize marketing campaigns by analyzing which content formats, channels, and messaging strategies resonate best with the target audience. For instance, AI can determine whether a particular product is better promoted through blog posts, social media, email marketing, or video content.

## Predictive Analytics for Affiliate Marketing Success

The next phase in leveraging AI for affiliate marketing is the use of predictive analytics. Predictive analytics involves using AI to analyze historical data and current market trends to make predictions about future outcomes.

In affiliate marketing, predictive analytics can forecast which products are likely to become popular, what kind of content will generate the most engagement, and which marketing strategies will yield the best results. This foresight allows affiliate marketers to stay ahead of the curve, adapting their strategies to align with predicted trends and consumer behaviors.

For example, AI can predict seasonal trends, helping affiliates to plan their marketing activities in advance. It can also identify emerging consumer interests, enabling affiliates to diversify their product offerings to tap into new markets.

## Case Studies of AI-Enhanced Affiliate Marketing Strategies

To illustrate the impact of AI in affiliate marketing, let's examine some case studies of successful AI-enhanced strategies.

- **Case Study 1: AI-Driven Product Selection** An affiliate marketer specializing in tech gadgets used AI to analyze market trends and consumer reviews. The AI system identified a set of emerging tech products that were gaining popularity but were not yet widely promoted by other affiliates. By focusing on these products, the affiliate was able to capitalize on the market gap, resulting in increased sales and commission.
- **Case Study 2: Optimizing Marketing Campaigns with AI** A fashion blogger used AI tools to analyze her audience's engagement across different content formats. The AI revealed that video content and Instagram posts generated the most engagement and conversions for fashion products. By focusing her efforts on these formats, the blogger significantly increased her affiliate marketing revenue.

- **Case Study 3: Predictive Analytics in Action** An online education platform utilized AI for predictive analytics to understand future trends in e-learning. The AI tools predicted a surge in demand for courses in data science and programming. The platform adjusted its affiliate marketing strategy to focus on these courses, resulting in a substantial increase in enrollments and affiliate earnings.

## The Future of AI in Affiliate Marketing

As we look to the future, the integration of AI in affiliate marketing is set to deepen. We can expect even more sophisticated AI tools that offer greater insights and predictive capabilities. The use of AI in personalizing affiliate marketing efforts to individual consumers will also become more prevalent.

However, this future also brings challenges. Ensuring ethical use of AI, maintaining transparency in AI-driven recommendations, and balancing AI strategies with human intuition and creativity will be crucial.

## Conclusion

The story of AI in affiliate marketing is one of innovation, efficiency, and forward-thinking strategies. From selecting and promoting products to utilizing predictive analytics for success, AI has not just improved existing processes but has opened new possibilities for growth and effectiveness in affiliate marketing. As AI continues to evolve, it will undoubtedly shape the future of this field, offering more intelligent, efficient, and personalized ways to connect products with consumers. For affiliate marketers, embracing AI is key to staying competitive and successful in the ever-changing digital landscape.

# CREATING AI-POWERED DIGITAL PRODUCTS

In the rapidly evolving digital landscape, Artificial Intelligence (AI) has become a cornerstone in the development of innovative and impactful digital products. This story explores the journey of developing AI-based apps and tools, devising monetization strategies, and the crucial role of market research and user feedback in shaping successful AI products.

## Developing AI-Based Apps and Tools

The first chapter in our exploration of AI-powered digital products begins with the development process. Creating an AI-based app or tool is a journey that intertwines advanced technology with creative problem-solving.

The development process typically starts with identifying a problem or a need in the market that can be addressed with AI.

This could range from automating mundane tasks to providing sophisticated data analysis or even enhancing user experiences through personalized interactions.

Once the problem is identified, the next step is choosing the right AI technology to address it. This involves decisions about using machine learning, natural language processing, computer vision, or other AI technologies. The choice depends on the nature of the problem and the type of solution envisioned.

The development phase involves training the AI model with relevant data, ensuring it can perform its intended function accurately and efficiently. This phase is iterative, involving continuous testing and refinement of the AI algorithms.

For instance, developing an AI-based health monitoring app would involve training the AI with vast amounts of health-related data, ensuring it can accurately interpret symptoms and provide reliable health advice or diagnostics.

## Monetization Strategies for AI Products

Once the AI product is developed, the next chapter focuses on monetization strategies. The digital market is competitive, and finding the right monetization model is crucial for the product's success.

There are various monetization strategies for AI-powered products, including subscription models, freemium models, in-app purchases, and advertising. The choice of monetization strategy depends on the product type, target audience, and market dynamics.

Subscription models work well for products that offer ongoing value, such as AI-driven analytics tools or productivity apps. Freemium models, where the basic features are free but advanced features are paid, can be effective for products that have a wide potential user base. In-app purchases and advertising are other viable strategies, particularly for consumer-focused apps.

## Market Research and User Feedback in Product Development

The final piece of the AI product development puzzle is market research and user feedback. Understanding the market and the target users is crucial for developing a product that meets real needs and gains traction in the market.

Market research involves analyzing market trends, competitor products, and potential user demographics. This research provides insights into what features are in demand, what gaps exist in the market, and how to position the product effectively.

User feedback is equally important. Engaging with early users, gathering feedback, and iterating the product based on this feedback is essential for refining the product and ensuring it meets user expectations. This feedback loop can involve beta testing, user surveys, and analyzing user behavior within the app.

For example, if the AI health monitoring app receives feedback that users find certain diagnostics confusing, the developers can refine the AI algorithms or the user interface to make it more user-friendly and accurate.

## The Future of AI-Powered Digital Products

Looking to the future, the development of AI-powered digital products is set to become more sophisticated and user-centric. Advancements in AI technology will enable the creation of more powerful and intuitive apps and tools. The integration of AI with other emerging technologies like augmented reality and the Internet of Things will open new avenues for innovation.

However, this future also brings challenges. Navigating the ethical implications of AI, ensuring user privacy and data security, and staying ahead of rapidly evolving technology trends will be crucial.

## *Conclusion*

The story of creating AI-powered digital products is one of innovation, strategic planning, and continuous adaptation. From developing AI-based apps and tools to devising effective monetization strategies and incorporating market research and user feedback, the journey is complex but rewarding. As AI continues to advance, it will undoubtedly shape the future of digital product development, offering more intelligent, efficient, and user-friendly solutions. For developers and entrepreneurs, embracing AI is key to creating digital products that not only succeed in the market but also make a meaningful impact on users' lives

# MAXIMIZING ONLINE ADVERTISING WITH AI

In the dynamic world of digital marketing, Artificial Intelligence (AI) has become a pivotal tool in reshaping online advertising strategies. This story explores the integration of AI in ad targeting and placement, budget optimization, ROI analysis, A/B testing, and ad performance tracking, painting a picture of a future where AI not only enhances but redefines online advertising.

## AI Algorithms for Ad Targeting and Placement

The first chapter in our AI-driven online advertising story begins with ad targeting and placement. Traditional online advertising often relied on broad targeting parameters and sometimes guesswork. AI, however, brings precision and efficiency to this process.

AI algorithms analyze vast amounts of data to understand consumer behaviors, preferences, and patterns. This data-driven approach allows for hyper-targeted ad campaigns that reach the most relevant audience segments. For instance, AI can identify potential customers based on their browsing history, purchase history, and even social media activity.

Moreover, AI optimizes ad placement to ensure maximum visibility and engagement. By analyzing data on user engagement across different platforms and times of the day, AI determines the most effective channels and times for ad placement. This ensures that ads are not only seen by the right audience but also at the right time and in the right context.

## Budget Optimization and ROI Analysis

The next phase in leveraging AI for online advertising is budget optimization and ROI analysis. One of the biggest challenges in advertising is allocating the budget in a way that maximizes return on investment (ROI). AI revolutionizes this aspect by providing more accurate and dynamic budget allocation.

AI algorithms can predict the performance of different advertising strategies and allocate the budget accordingly. They continuously analyze campaign performance data, adjusting the budget in real-time to focus on the most effective strategies. This dynamic approach ensures that the advertising budget is used efficiently, maximizing ROI.

AI also enhances ROI analysis by providing deeper insights into campaign performance. Beyond basic metrics like click-through rates and conversions, AI can track and analyze the long-term value of customers acquired through advertising, providing a more comprehensive view of ROI.

## A/B Testing and Ad Performance
### Tracking with AI

The final piece of the AI in online advertising puzzle is A/B testing and ad performance tracking. A/B testing, a method of comparing two versions of an ad to determine which performs better, is crucial for optimizing ad campaigns. AI takes A/B testing to a new level.

AI-driven A/B testing involves not just simple comparison but deep analysis of various elements of the ads, such as messaging, visuals, and call-to-action buttons. AI can run multiple tests simultaneously and analyze the results more quickly and accurately than manual methods.

Ad performance tracking with AI involves continuous monitoring and analysis of ad campaigns. AI tools track a wide range of performance metrics and use machine learning to identify patterns and insights that can inform future campaigns. This level of analysis helps advertisers understand what works and what doesn't, refining their strategies for better results.

## The Future of AI in Online Advertising

As we look to the future, the role of AI in online advertising is set to grow even more significant. With advancements in AI technology, we can expect even more sophisticated tools for ad targeting, budget optimization, and performance analysis. The integration of AI with emerging technologies like augmented reality and programmatic advertising will further enhance the capabilities of online advertising.

However, this future also brings challenges. Ensuring data privacy and ethical use of AI in advertising, as well as keeping up with rapidly evolving technology, will be crucial for advertisers.

## Conclusion

The story of AI in online advertising is one of transformation, efficiency, and continuous evolution. From enhancing ad targeting and placement to optimizing budgets and analyzing ROI, AI has not just improved existing processes but has opened new avenues for innovation and success in advertising. As AI continues to evolve, it will undoubtedly shape the future of online advertising, offering more intelligent, efficient, and effective ways to connect with audiences. For advertisers and marketers, mastering AI is no longer an option but a necessity to stay competitive in the ever-changing landscape of digital marketing.

# BUILDING AN AI-FRIENDLY WEBSITE

In the digital era, where websites serve as the digital storefronts for businesses and individuals alike, Artificial Intelligence (AI) has become a crucial element in creating engaging, dynamic, and personalized user experiences. This story delves into the nuances of designing AI-driven user experiences, implementing AI for dynamic content and personalization, and the tools and best practices for AI integration in website development.

## Designing AI-Driven User Experiences

The first chapter in our AI-friendly website story begins with the design of AI-driven user experiences. The goal of integrating AI into website design is to create an intuitive, engaging, and seamless experience for users. This involves understanding user behavior, preferences, and needs, and using AI to cater to these aspects dynamically.

AI-driven design starts with data. By analyzing user data, AI can identify patterns and preferences, which can inform the design process. For instance, AI can determine the most effective layout, color scheme, and navigation based on user interactions and engagement metrics.

Moreover, AI can enhance user experience through intelligent features like chatbots that provide instant customer service, voice assistants that offer hands-free navigation, and recommendation engines that suggest content or products based on user preferences.

## Implementing AI for Dynamic Content and Personalization

The next phase in building an AI-friendly website is implementing AI for dynamic content creation and personalization. Personalization is key in today's digital landscape, where users expect content that is relevant and tailored to their interests.

AI algorithms can analyze user data in real-time to deliver personalized content. This could be in the form of personalized product recommendations in an e-commerce store, customized content feeds in a news portal, or individualized user interfaces.

Dynamic content creation with AI involves the website adapting its content and structure based on user interactions. For example, an AI system can change the layout of a homepage based on the time of day, user location, or user behavior from previous visits.

## Tools and Best Practices for AI Integration

The final chapter in our story focuses on the tools and best practices for AI integration in website development. The market offers a plethora of tools and platforms that facilitate AI integration, ranging from AI-powered web development platforms to specialized AI services for personalization, analytics, and customer service.

Choosing the right tools depends on the specific needs and goals of the website. For instance, platforms like TensorFlow or IBM Watson offer AI services that can be integrated into websites for various purposes, from data analysis to natural language processing.

Best practices for AI integration include:

- **Data Privacy and Security**: Ensuring user data is handled securely and ethically is paramount. This involves transparent data collection policies and robust security measures to protect user data.
- **User-Centric Design**: AI integration should always aim to enhance user experience. This means avoiding overly intrusive personalization or features that might detract from the user experience.
- **Continuous Testing and Iteration**: AI systems require continuous monitoring and refinement. Regular testing and updating are essential to ensure the AI components of the website are performing as intended and improving over time.
- **Balancing AI and Human Elements**: While AI can greatly enhance a website, it's important to maintain a balance between automated AI elements and human touches. This could mean having human customer service representatives available alongside AI chatbots.

## The Future of AI-Friendly Websites

Looking to the future, AI-friendly websites are set to become more sophisticated and intuitive. Advancements in AI technology will enable more advanced personalization, dynamic content creation, and user interaction capabilities. The integration of AI with other emerging technologies like augmented reality (AR) and the Internet of Things (IoT) will further expand the possibilities for innovative website experiences.

However, this future also brings challenges. Keeping up with rapidly evolving AI technology, ensuring ethical use of AI, and maintaining a focus on user-centric design will be crucial for developers and businesses alike.

## Conclusion

The story of building an AI-friendly website is one of innovation, user-centric design, and continuous adaptation. From designing AI-driven user experiences to implementing AI for dynamic content and personalization, and choosing the right tools and best practices for AI integration, the journey is complex but rewarding. As AI continues to advance, it will undoubtedly shape the future of website development, offering more intelligent, efficient, and personalized user experiences. For website developers and businesses, embracing AI is key to creating digital platforms that not only attract and retain users but also provide them with a unique and engaging experience.

# AI IN VIDEO PRODUCTION AND YOUTUBE MONETIZATION

In the vibrant world of digital content, where video reigns supreme, Artificial Intelligence (AI) has emerged as a transformative force in video production and YouTube monetization. This story unfolds the role of AI in editing and enhancing videos, driving YouTube SEO strategies, and optimizing video content for better monetization.

## AI Tools for Editing and Enhancing Videos

The first chapter in our AI-driven video production story begins with the tools that are reshaping how videos are edited and enhanced. Traditional video editing is a time-consuming process, requiring a high level of skill and effort. AI, however, brings efficiency and innovation to this process.

AI-powered video editing tools can automate various aspects of the editing process, from color correction to sound design. These tools use machine learning algorithms to analyze footage and apply enhancements automatically. For instance, AI can stabilize shaky footage, adjust lighting and color balance, and even edit out unwanted segments.

Beyond basic editing, AI also offers advanced features like object recognition and automated tagging, making it easier to organize and search through footage. AI can also generate subtitles and closed captions, not only saving time but also enhancing accessibility.

## AI-Driven Strategies for YouTube SEO

The next phase in leveraging AI for YouTube success focuses on SEO strategies. In the crowded space of YouTube, getting your videos to stand out and reach the right audience is crucial. AI plays a pivotal role in optimizing videos for YouTube's search algorithms.

AI-driven SEO tools analyze various factors that influence YouTube rankings, such as video titles, descriptions, tags, and even the content of the video itself. These tools can suggest keywords, identify trending topics, and provide insights on how to structure video content for better visibility.

For example, AI can analyze the performance of similar videos on YouTube to suggest the most effective keywords and topics. It can also track changes in YouTube's algorithm, helping creators adapt their strategies to maintain high visibility.

## *Analyzing and Optimizing Video Content for Better Monetization*

The final piece of the AI in video production and monetization puzzle is the analysis and optimization of video content. Monetizing YouTube content effectively requires a deep understanding of what resonates with audiences and drives engagement.

AI tools can analyze viewer behavior, engagement metrics, and performance trends to provide insights into what makes a video successful. This includes analysis of watch time, viewer demographics, and engagement patterns like likes, comments, and shares.

Based on this analysis, AI can suggest content tweaks to improve engagement and retention, which are key factors in YouTube's monetization algorithms. For instance, AI can identify the most engaging parts of a video or suggest the best moments for inserting ads.

Moreover, AI can help in optimizing video content for different platforms beyond YouTube, ensuring that creators maximize their reach and monetization potential across the digital landscape.

## The Future of AI in Video Production and YouTube Monetization

As we look to the future, the integration of AI in video production and YouTube monetization is set to become even more sophisticated. We can expect advancements in AI technology to lead to more powerful editing tools, more accurate SEO strategies, and deeper insights into video performance.

However, this future also brings challenges. Keeping up with rapidly evolving AI technology, ensuring ethical use of AI, and balancing AI-driven strategies with creative content creation will be crucial for video creators and marketers.

## Conclusion

The story of AI in video production and YouTube monetization is one of innovation, efficiency, and strategic insight. From AI tools that revolutionize video editing to AI-driven strategies for YouTube SEO, and the analysis and optimization of video content for better monetization, AI has not just improved existing processes but has opened new possibilities for success in the digital content arena. As AI continues to advance, it will undoubtedly shape the future of video production and content monetization, offering more intelligent, efficient, and effective ways to create and monetize video content. For content creators and marketers, embracing AI is key to staying competitive and successful in the ever-evolving world of digital video.

# AUTOMATION AND SCALING: GROWING YOUR ONLINE BUSINESS

In the fast-paced digital economy, businesses constantly seek ways to grow and stay competitive. Artificial Intelligence (AI) has emerged as a key player in this quest, offering innovative solutions for automation and scaling. This story explores the journey of using AI for business process automation, strategies for scaling up with AI technology, and the crucial balance between automation and the human touch.

## Using AI for Business Process Automation

The first chapter in our story of business growth and AI begins with business process automation. In the digital age, efficiency and speed are paramount, and AI provides tools to achieve both by automating routine and time-consuming tasks.

AI-driven automation involves using machine learning algorithms, natural language processing, and other AI technologies to handle tasks that traditionally required human intervention. This includes customer service inquiries handled by AI chatbots, automated inventory management systems, and AI-driven analytics for market research and data analysis.

For example, an e-commerce business can use AI to automate its customer service, with chatbots handling common inquiries and issues. This not only speeds up response times but also frees up human customer service representatives to handle more complex issues.

## Strategies for Scaling Up with AI Technology

The next phase in our narrative focuses on strategies for scaling up businesses using AI technology. Scaling a business involves more than just increasing sales; it requires expanding operational capacity and efficiency.

AI technology plays a crucial role in this scaling process. It can analyze vast amounts of data to identify growth opportunities, optimize marketing strategies, and streamline operations. AI-driven tools can also predict market trends, helping businesses to adapt and scale their operations proactively.

For instance, AI can help an online retailer identify which products are likely to be in high demand, allowing them to adjust their inventory and marketing strategies accordingly. AI can also optimize logistics and supply chain management, ensuring that the business can handle increased order volumes efficiently.

## *Balancing Automation with Human Touch*

The final chapter in our story addresses the balance between automation and the human touch. While AI and automation offer numerous benefits, maintaining a human element in certain aspects of the business is crucial for success.

This balance is particularly important in areas like customer service and sales. While AI can handle routine inquiries and processes, human interaction is often necessary for complex issues or high-value sales negotiations. The key is to use AI to enhance, not replace, human skills and interactions.

For example, while a chatbot can handle initial customer inquiries, complex issues can be escalated to a human representative. Similarly, AI can assist sales teams by providing data-driven insights and lead scoring, but the actual sales process may still rely on human interaction and relationship building.

## The Future of Automation and Scaling in Online Business

Looking to the future, the role of AI in business automation and scaling is set to grow even more significant. We can expect advancements in AI technology to lead to more sophisticated automation solutions, enabling businesses to scale up more efficiently and effectively.

However, this future also brings challenges. Keeping up with rapidly evolving AI technology, ensuring ethical use of AI, and maintaining the right balance between automation and human interaction will be crucial for businesses.

## Conclusion

The story of automation and scaling in online business through AI is one of innovation, strategic growth, and the harmonious integration of technology and human skills. From using AI for business process automation to developing strategies for scaling up and balancing automation with the human touch, AI has not just improved existing processes but has opened new avenues for business growth and efficiency. As AI continues to advance, it will undoubtedly shape the future of online business, offering more intelligent, efficient, and effective ways to grow and compete in the digital marketplace. For businesses, embracing AI while maintaining a focus on the human aspects of their operations is key to sustainable growth and success.

# ETHICAL CONSIDERATIONS IN AI FOR BUSINESS

In the rapidly evolving world of business technology, Artificial Intelligence (AI) stands at the forefront, offering unparalleled opportunities for growth and efficiency. However, with great power comes great responsibility, and the integration of AI in business brings a host of ethical considerations that must be navigated with care. This story delves into the ethical implications of AI in business, the importance of data privacy and security, and the responsible use of AI in marketing and customer interactions.

## Discussing the Ethical Implications of AI in Business

The first chapter in our exploration of AI ethics begins with a broad overview of the ethical implications of AI in the business world. AI, with its ability to analyze vast amounts of data and make decisions, poses unique ethical challenges. These include concerns about bias, transparency, accountability, and the potential impact on employment.

One of the primary ethical concerns is the issue of bias in AI algorithms. AI systems are only as unbiased as the data they are trained on, and if this data contains biases, the AI's decisions will reflect them. This can lead to unfair or discriminatory outcomes, particularly in areas like hiring, lending, and customer service.

Transparency and accountability are also major ethical considerations. Businesses must ensure that their AI systems' decision-making processes are transparent and that there is accountability for the decisions made by AI. This is crucial not only for ethical reasons but also for maintaining trust with customers and stakeholders.

## Ensuring Data Privacy and Security

The next phase of our narrative focuses on data privacy and security, a critical aspect of ethical AI implementation. In the age of big data, businesses have access to vast amounts of personal information, and AI systems often rely on this data to function. Ensuring the privacy and security of this data is not just a legal obligation but an ethical one.

Data privacy concerns revolve around how data is collected, used, and shared. Businesses must ensure that they have explicit consent to use personal data, that the data is used only for its intended purpose, and that it is not shared without permission.

Data security is equally important. AI systems must be designed with robust security measures to protect against data breaches and cyber attacks. This includes not only technical safeguards but also employee training and policies to prevent human error, which is a common cause of data breaches.

## *Responsible Use of AI in Marketing and Customer Interactions*

The final chapter in our AI ethics story addresses the responsible use of AI in marketing and customer interactions. AI offers powerful tools for personalized marketing, but these must be used responsibly to avoid invading privacy or manipulating customers.

Responsible AI marketing involves being transparent about the use of AI, such as informing customers when they are interacting with a chatbot. It also means using AI to enhance the customer experience without being intrusive or manipulative.

For example, AI can be used to personalize product recommendations based on a customer's past purchases and preferences, but it should not be used to exploit vulnerabilities or push customers to make decisions that are not in their best interest.

Balancing personalization with privacy is key. Businesses must ensure that they are not crossing the line from helpful personalization into invasive surveillance.

## The Future of Ethical AI in Business

Looking to the future, the ethical considerations of AI in business will become even more important as AI technology continues to advance. Businesses will need to stay vigilant about emerging ethical challenges and adapt their policies and practices accordingly.

However, this future also offers hope. As awareness of AI ethics grows, we can expect more robust frameworks for ethical AI, both from regulatory bodies and within businesses themselves.

## Conclusion

The story of ethical considerations in AI for business is one of ongoing vigilance, adaptation, and commitment to doing what is right. From navigating the ethical implications of AI decision-making to ensuring data privacy and security, and responsibly using AI in marketing and customer interactions, the journey is complex but essential. As AI continues to transform the business landscape, maintaining a strong ethical foundation will be key to harnessing the power of AI for good. For businesses, this means not only embracing AI's potential but also committing to its responsible and ethical use

# AI TOOLS AND RESOURCES FOR ENTREPRENEURS

In the entrepreneurial world, where innovation and efficiency are key to success, Artificial Intelligence (AI) has emerged as a vital ally. This story unfolds the plethora of AI tools and platforms available to entrepreneurs, the resources for learning and staying updated on AI trends, and the community and support systems that bolster AI entrepreneurship.

## Comprehensive List of AI Tools and Platforms

The first chapter in our exploration of AI tools and resources begins with a comprehensive look at the AI tools and platforms available to entrepreneurs. These tools span various business needs, from automating routine tasks to providing sophisticated data analysis and enhancing customer experiences.

- **AI for Data Analysis and Business Intelligence**: Tools like Tableau, IBM Watson, and Google Analytics use AI to provide deep insights into business data. They help entrepreneurs make data-driven decisions by analyzing market trends, customer behavior, and operational efficiency.

- **AI for Marketing and Customer Engagement**: Platforms like Marketo and HubSpot leverage AI to personalize marketing campaigns and optimize customer engagement strategies. They analyze customer data to tailor marketing messages and predict the most effective marketing channels.
- **AI for Customer Service**: Chatbots and virtual assistants powered by AI, such as Drift and Intercom, provide automated customer support. They handle routine inquiries, freeing up human customer service representatives to deal with more complex issues.
- **AI for Financial Management**: Tools like QuickBooks and Xero use AI to automate financial tasks such as invoicing, payroll, and expense tracking. They provide entrepreneurs with real-time insights into their financial health.
- **AI for E-commerce**: Platforms like Shopify and BigCommerce integrate AI to offer personalized shopping experiences, recommend products, and manage inventory efficiently.

## *Resources for Learning and Staying Updated on AI Trends*

The next phase in our narrative focuses on resources for learning about AI and staying abreast of the latest trends. For entrepreneurs, understanding AI and its evolving landscape is crucial to leveraging its full potential.

- **Online Courses and Tutorials**: Websites like Coursera, Udemy, and edX offer courses on AI and machine learning, catering to various skill levels. These courses are often created by leading universities and tech companies, providing high-quality, structured learning.

- **Books and Publications**: Reading books and publications is another excellent way to learn about AI. Titles like "Artificial Intelligence: A Guide for Thinking Humans" by Melanie Mitchell and "Life 3.0: Being Human in the Age of Artificial Intelligence" by Max Tegmark offer insightful perspectives on AI.
- **Blogs and News Sites**: Staying updated with blogs and news sites focused on AI, such as TechCrunch, VentureBeat, and the AI section of MIT Technology Review, is essential for keeping up with the latest trends and developments.
- **Podcasts and Webinars**: Podcasts like "AI in Business" and "The AI Alignment Podcast" and webinars hosted by AI experts and organizations offer a convenient way to stay informed and gain insights from industry leaders.

## Community and Support Systems for AI Entrepreneurs

The final chapter in our AI tools and resources story highlights the importance of community and support systems for AI entrepreneurs. Navigating the AI landscape can be challenging, and a supportive community can make a significant difference.

- **Online Forums and Social Media Groups**: Platforms like LinkedIn, Reddit, and specialized online forums host vibrant communities of AI enthusiasts and professionals. These communities are valuable for networking, sharing knowledge, and seeking advice.
- **Incubators and Accelerators**: AI-focused incubators and accelerators, such as Y Combinator and Techstars, provide mentorship, resources, and funding opportunities for AI startups. They also offer a community of fellow entrepreneurs and industry

experts.

- **Conferences and Meetups**: Attending AI conferences and local meetups is a great way to connect with other AI entrepreneurs, learn from experts, and stay updated on industry trends. Events like the AI Summit and NeurIPS offer opportunities for learning and networking.

## The Future of AI Tools and Resources for Entrepreneurs

Looking to the future, the landscape of AI tools and resources for entrepreneurs is set to become even more diverse and accessible. We can expect advancements in AI technology to lead to more sophisticated tools, making AI more powerful and easier to use for entrepreneurs.

However, this future also brings challenges. Keeping up with rapidly evolving AI technology, understanding the ethical implications of AI, and choosing the right tools from an ever-growing pool will be crucial for entrepreneurs.

## Conclusion

The story of AI tools and resources for entrepreneurs is one of empowerment, continuous learning, and community support. From a wide array of AI tools that cater to various business needs to resources for learning and staying updated on AI trends, and the supportive community and networks, the journey is rich and rewarding. As AI continues to advance, it will undoubtedly shape the future of entrepreneurship, offering more intelligent, efficient, and effective tools and resources. For entrepreneurs, embracing AI while actively engaging in learning and community participation is key to harnessing the power of AI for business success

# FUTURE TRENDS: AI AND EMERGING DIGITAL MARKETS

In the rapidly evolving world of technology, Artificial Intelligence (AI) stands as a beacon of progress and innovation. As we look towards the future, AI's influence on business and emerging digital markets becomes a captivating narrative, filled with predictions, emerging niches, and strategies for adaptation. This story delves into the future landscape of AI in business, the burgeoning markets in the AI space, and how businesses can prepare for the upcoming changes and advancements in AI.

## Predicting the Future Landscape
## of AI in Business

The first chapter in our exploration of AI's future begins with predictions about how AI will shape the business world. AI, already a transformative force, is poised to become even more integral in various business operations, decision-making processes, and customer interactions.

- **AI in Decision Making**: AI's role in business decision-making is expected to grow exponentially. With advancements in predictive analytics and machine learning, AI will provide businesses with deeper insights and foresight, aiding in more informed and strategic decision-making processes.
- **Customization and Personalization**: AI will drive unprecedented levels of customization in products and services. Businesses will use AI to understand and predict individual customer preferences, delivering highly personalized experiences.
- **Operational Efficiency**: AI will continue to streamline business operations, reducing costs and increasing efficiency. From supply chain management to resource allocation, AI's ability to optimize complex systems will be invaluable.
- **Ethical AI and Governance**: As AI becomes more pervasive, the focus on ethical AI and governance will intensify. Businesses will need to address concerns around bias, transparency, and accountability in AI systems.

## Emerging Markets and Niches in the AI Space

The next phase of our narrative focuses on the emerging markets and niches within the AI space. As AI technology advances, new markets are opening up, offering opportunities for innovation and growth.

- **Healthcare AI**: One of the most promising areas is AI in healthcare. From diagnostics to personalized treatment plans and drug discovery, AI is set to revolutionize the healthcare industry.
- **AI in Education**: AI is transforming the education

sector, offering personalized learning experiences, automating administrative tasks, and providing tools for educators and students.

- **Sustainable AI for Environmental Solutions**: AI is being leveraged to address environmental challenges. This includes everything from climate modeling and renewable energy optimization to wildlife conservation.
- **AI in Financial Services**: The financial sector will see increased AI integration for fraud detection, risk assessment, automated trading, and personalized financial planning.

## Preparing for Upcoming Changes and Advancements in AI

The final chapter in our AI future story addresses how businesses can prepare for the upcoming changes and advancements in AI. Staying ahead in the AI curve requires strategic planning, continuous learning, and adaptability.

- **Investing in AI Skills and Talent**: Businesses must invest in AI skills and talent. This includes training current employees and hiring new talent with AI expertise.
- **Staying Informed and Agile**: Keeping abreast of the latest AI developments and being agile in implementing new technologies will be crucial. Businesses should stay connected with AI communities, attend conferences, and engage with thought leaders.
- **Ethical AI Implementation**: As businesses adopt more AI solutions, implementing these technologies ethically and responsibly will be paramount. This includes

ensuring data privacy, addressing bias in AI algorithms, and being transparent about AI use.

- **Collaboration and Partnerships**: Collaborating with AI startups, academic institutions, and other businesses can provide access to new AI technologies and insights. Partnerships will be key in navigating the AI landscape.

## The Future of AI and Emerging Digital Markets

Looking to the future, AI's role in shaping business and emerging digital markets is set to be profound and far-reaching. The advancements in AI will open new avenues for innovation, efficiency, and personalized services. However, this future also brings challenges, including ethical considerations, the need for skilled AI professionals, and the continuous evolution of technology.

## Conclusion

The story of AI and emerging digital markets is one of continuous evolution, opportunity, and strategic foresight. From predicting the future landscape of AI in business to identifying emerging markets and preparing for upcoming changes, the journey is complex but filled with potential. As AI continues to advance, it will undoubtedly shape the future of business and technology, offering new opportunities for growth and innovation. For businesses, staying informed, adaptable, and ethically grounded in AI practices is key to thriving in this new era.

# CASE STUDIES: SUCCESS STORIES IN AI AND ONLINE BUSINESS

In the digital age, Artificial Intelligence (AI) has become a catalyst for innovation and success in online business. This story unfolds through real-world examples of businesses that have harnessed AI to transform their operations, the lessons learned from these successful AI applications, and the inspiration they provide for implementing AI across various business models.

## Real-World Examples of Businesses Succeeding with AI

The first chapter of our story begins with a dive into real-world examples where AI has been a game-changer for businesses.

- **E-commerce Personalization - The Amazon Success Story**: Amazon's use of AI in personalizing shopping experiences is a classic example. The company uses machine learning algorithms to analyze customer data, including past purchases, search history, and browsing behavior. This analysis powers their recommendation engine, suggesting products that customers are likely to purchase. This AI-driven personalization has significantly increased Amazon's sales and customer loyalty.

- **AI in Customer Service - The Zappos Approach**: Zappos, an online shoe and clothing retailer, implemented AI in their customer service with impressive results. They used chatbots to handle routine customer inquiries, freeing up human agents to deal with more complex issues. This not only improved efficiency but also enhanced customer satisfaction through quicker response times.
- **Content Creation - The Forbes Experiment**: Forbes incorporated an AI tool named Bertie to assist in content creation and editorial planning. Bertie suggests article topics based on trending news and provides reporters with first drafts, which are then refined by human editors. This integration of AI has streamlined Forbes' content creation process, making it more efficient and responsive to current events.

## Lessons Learned and Insights from Successful AI Applications

The next phase of our narrative focuses on the lessons learned and insights gained from these successful AI applications.

- **Data is Key in AI Implementation**: One of the primary lessons from Amazon's success is the importance of data. AI systems require large datasets to learn and make accurate predictions. Collecting and analyzing customer data was crucial in Amazon's ability to personalize shopping experiences effectively.
- **Balancing AI and Human Interaction**: Zappos' approach highlights the importance of balancing AI automation

with human interaction. While AI can handle routine tasks efficiently, the human touch is essential for dealing with complex issues and providing a personal customer service experience.

- **AI as a Collaborative Tool**: Forbes' use of Bertie demonstrates that AI can be a powerful collaborator rather than a replacement for human skills. AI can handle certain tasks, like initial data analysis or draft creation, allowing human employees to focus on more creative and strategic activities.

## Inspiration and Ideas for Implementing AI in Various Business Models

The final chapter in our story provides inspiration and ideas for implementing AI across various business models.

- **AI in Small Businesses**: Small businesses can use AI for customer segmentation and targeted marketing. AI tools can analyze customer data to identify distinct segments and tailor marketing messages to each group, making marketing efforts more effective and efficient.
- **AI in Healthcare Services**: Online healthcare platforms can use AI for preliminary diagnostics and patient triage. AI algorithms can analyze patient symptoms and medical history to provide preliminary diagnoses, improving the efficiency of healthcare delivery.
- **AI in Education Platforms**: Online education platforms can leverage AI for personalized learning experiences. AI can analyze a student's learning style and progress to suggest customized learning paths and resources, enhancing the effectiveness of online learning.

## The Future of AI in Online Business

Looking to the future, the role of AI in online business is set to become even more significant. We can expect advancements in AI technology to lead to more sophisticated applications, offering new opportunities for innovation and efficiency.

However, this future also brings challenges. Keeping up with rapidly evolving AI technology, ensuring ethical use of AI, and finding the right balance between AI automation and human interaction will be crucial for businesses.

## Conclusion

The story of AI in online business, as told through these case studies, is one of innovation, efficiency, and strategic insight. From e-commerce personalization to AI in customer service and content creation, AI has not just improved existing processes but has opened new avenues for success in the digital world. As AI continues to advance, it will undoubtedly shape the future of online business, offering more intelligent, efficient, and effective ways to operate and grow. For businesses, embracing AI while learning from these success stories is key to navigating the digital landscape and achieving success.

# YOUR AI ACTION PLAN: STEPS TO PROFIT ONLINE

In the digital era, where competition is fierce and technology evolves rapidly, Artificial Intelligence (AI) has become a key differentiator for online businesses. This story outlines a strategic plan for implementing AI, setting goals and milestones, and tips for ongoing improvement in the AI landscape, guiding businesses towards profitability and success.

## Creating a Strategic Plan for Implementing AI

The first chapter of our AI action plan story begins with the creation of a strategic plan for AI implementation. This plan is the roadmap that guides businesses through the complexities of AI integration and ensures that the technology aligns with business objectives.

- **Assessing Business Needs and AI Readiness**: The first step involves assessing the business's specific needs and how AI can address them. This includes analyzing current operations, identifying areas where AI can add value, and evaluating the business's readiness for AI integration in terms of infrastructure, data availability, and skill sets.

- **Researching AI Solutions**: Once the needs are identified, the next step is researching AI solutions that fit these requirements. This involves exploring different AI technologies, platforms, and tools, and understanding their capabilities and limitations.
- **Developing an AI Roadmap**: With a clear understanding of needs and solutions, businesses can develop an AI roadmap. This roadmap outlines the steps for AI implementation, including technology acquisition, team training, data preparation, and system integration.

## Setting Goals and Milestones for AI Integration

The next phase in our narrative focuses on setting clear goals and milestones for AI integration. These goals provide direction and measurable targets for the AI initiative.

- **Defining Clear Objectives**: The objectives of AI integration should be specific, measurable, achievable, relevant, and time-bound (SMART). For example, a goal could be to reduce customer service response times by 30% within six months using AI chatbots.
- **Establishing Milestones**: Breaking down the AI integration process into smaller, manageable milestones helps in tracking progress and maintaining momentum. Milestones could include completing AI training for staff, integrating AI into one business process, or achieving a specific performance metric.
- **Regular Review and Adjustment**: Setting regular intervals for reviewing progress towards goals and

milestones is crucial. This allows businesses to adjust their strategies in response to challenges or changes in the AI landscape.

## Tips for Ongoing Improvement and Adaptation in the AI Landscape

The final chapter in our AI action plan story provides tips for ongoing improvement and adaptation in the ever-evolving AI landscape.

- **Staying Informed on AI Trends**: The AI field is rapidly evolving, and staying informed on the latest trends and developments is essential. This can be achieved through continuous learning, attending industry conferences, and engaging with AI communities.
- **Encouraging a Culture of Innovation**: Fostering a culture of innovation within the organization encourages team members to explore new AI applications and improvements. This involves encouraging experimentation, providing training opportunities, and rewarding innovative ideas.
- **Monitoring AI Performance and Impact**: Regularly monitoring the performance of AI systems and their impact on business operations is key. This involves not just tracking technical performance but also assessing how AI is affecting customer experiences, employee productivity, and overall business outcomes.
- **Ethical Consideration and Compliance**: As AI becomes more integral to business operations, ethical considerations and compliance with regulations become increasingly important. This includes ensuring data privacy, addressing bias in AI algorithms, and being

transparent about AI use.

## The Future of AI in Online Business

Looking to the future, the role of AI in online business is set to become even more significant. The advancements in AI will open new avenues for innovation, efficiency, and personalized services. However, this future also brings challenges, including ethical considerations, the need for skilled AI professionals, and the continuous evolution of technology.

## Conclusion

The story of creating and executing an AI action plan for online profitability is one of strategic planning, goal setting, and continuous adaptation. From assessing business needs and researching AI solutions to setting clear objectives and staying agile in the AI landscape, the journey is complex but filled with potential. As AI continues to advance, it will undoubtedly shape the future of online business, offering new opportunities for growth and innovation. For businesses, embracing AI while maintaining a focus on ethical practices and continuous learning is key to harnessing the power of AI for success.